D1356150

How to Survive a

MIDLIFE CRISIS

CLIVE WHICHELOW *and* **MIKE HASKINS**

ILLUSTRATIONS BY KATE ROCHESTER

summersdale

HOW TO SURVIVE A MIDLIFE CRISIS

An Hachette UK Company
www.hachette.co.uk

Summersdale Publishers Ltd
Part of Octopus Publishing Group Limited
Carmelite House
50 Victoria Embankment
LONDON
EC4Y 0DZ
UK

www.summersdale.com

Printed and bound in Malta

ISBN: 978-1-78685-050-8

Substantial discounts on bulk quantities of Summersdale books are available to corporations, professional associations and other organisations. For details contact general enquiries: telephone: +44 (0) 1243 771107 or email: enquiries@summersdale.com.

To....................................

From................................

Introduction

Well, the first thing to do is admit that you're going through a midlife crisis.

It's OK, your secret's safe with us. Others may have spotted those little warning signs: buying leather trousers, hankering after a souped-up sports car or a 1000-cc Harley Davidson. But you've explained them away. Leather trousers are so much easier to wipe clean when you spill your porridge on them; that two-seater sports car makes so much more sense when you're not having to convey the entire family to theme parks and zoos any more, and that big bad motorbike with the ape-hanger handlebars, well, er...

See, you're not convincing anyone are you? Not even yourself.

So, the first step in surviving a midlife crisis is to own up. Not 'fess up', note, as that looks like a desperate attempt to be down with the kids and speak in hip urban argot, which is a dead giveaway that you are going through an MLC. See, it doesn't sound so bad when you abbreviate it does it? It sounds like one of those gongs the Queen dishes out on her birthday. I've been awarded the MLC dontcha know?!

So, don't deny it, embrace it. In fact, if you embrace the thing hard enough you might just kill it at birth.

This little book will guide you, step by tentative step through the pitfalls, booby-traps and shark-infested waters that lay before you in the midlife crisis jungle.

Don't worry, we're going to get through this together, with or without leather trousers!

A midlife crisis usually only lasts between three and ten years – after that you can pass it off as senility

• • • • • • • • • •

Eighty per cent of middle-aged people suffer a midlife crisis; the other 20 per cent deny they are middle-aged

• • • • • • • • • •

Your musical ability will not suddenly increase the moment you spend a month's wages on an electric guitar or a piano

• • • • • • • • • •

An MLC can start from as young as 35 – which for some people is only just out of their extended teenage years

WAYS YOUR FRIENDS AND FAMILY MAY TRIGGER A MIDLIFE CRISIS

They point out how much you're beginning to resemble your parents

. . . .

You realise you kiss your dog more often than your partner

. . . .

Since you put that video of him on YouTube, your cat has been earning more than you

They buy you an exercise
bike for your birthday
(hint, hint!)

WHAT A MIDLIFE CRISIS MEANS FOR YOU

Trying to relive the fashions of your youth without actually having the same size body any more

. . . .

Spending six months' wages on a racing bike and Lycra that you will only use about twice a year

. . . .

Realising the only way you can turn a few heads is by driving past in a fancy new car

Feeling the need to wear a hat at all times
– even when you're at home in bed

. . . .

Having a pin-up of your favourite band
member as your computer screen saver

. . . .

Getting into facial contouring and
wondering if it works on bodies as well

GETTING READY
TO GO OUT
NOW INVOLVES
AN EXTENSIVE
RENOVATION
PROJECT

HOW TO MAKE YOUR MIDLIFE CRISIS FUN

Stop calling it a midlife crisis and start calling it Teenagehood Part Two

. . . .

Switch from your golden oldies radio station to online streaming

. . . .

Look on the humorous side of your midlife crisis – tell people you are making a satirical attack on ageing

Wear silly clothes
and behave in a
ridiculous manner –
if that's not what
you're doing already

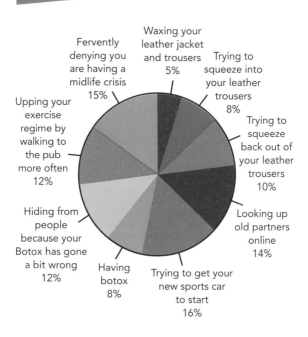

BREAKDOWN OF HOW YOU WILL SPEND YOUR TIME DURING YOUR MIDLIFE CRISIS

Fervently denying you are having a midlife crisis
15%

Waxing your leather jacket and trousers
5%

Trying to squeeze into your leather trousers
8%

Trying to squeeze back out of your leather trousers
10%

Upping your exercise regime by walking to the pub more often
12%

Looking up old partners online
14%

Hiding from people because your Botox has gone a bit wrong
12%

Having botox
8%

Trying to get your new sports car to start
16%

GOOD AND BAD NEWS ABOUT YOUR MIDLIFE CRISIS

GOOD NEWS	BAD NEWS
You feel like you're 18 again	You give up your job and have the same amount of money you had when you were 18
You rediscover a burst of youthful energy	Your bursts of youthful energy are followed by longer periods of middle-aged breathlessness
You finally have an excuse to act like someone half your age	People half your age will find this acutely embarrassing
All problems, failings and eccentric behaviour can now be blamed on your MLC	Unfortunately people will remember that you were like this before your MLC too

WAYS YOUR MIDLIFE CRISIS COULD AFFECT YOUR
HEALTH

You try so hard to keep fit you end up pulling every muscle in your body

If you try to drink the amount of alcohol
you regularly consumed 25 years ago,
you may miss the next 25 years

. . . .

The only way you are likely to
lose those extra pounds now is by
worrying about how fat you are

. . . .

You start wearing sunglasses to
hide the bags under your eyes
and keep walking into doors
because it's too dark to see

BATHROOM CUPBOARD ESSENTIALS TO HELP YOU THROUGH YOUR MIDLIFE CRISIS

Plentiful supplies of Deep Heat rub for aches and pains caused by climbing in and out of your sports car, overdoing it on the dance floor, etc.

* * * * * * * * * *

The rose-tinted spectacles through which all glances in the mirror will now take place

* * * * * * * * * *

Equal quantities of hair remover and hair-restorer – who said your MLC wouldn't be full of such little ironies?

FANTASIES AND REALITY OF A MIDLIFE CRISIS

FANTASY	REALITY
You give up your job and become free	You give up your job and become free of any idea what to do
You can go to music festivals and spend all weekend watching your favourite bands	You go to music festivals and spend all weekend queuing for the Portaloo
You're a role model	You're a roly-poly model
You have aged pretty well	You have aged. Pretty? Well…

HOW LONG WILL YOUR MIDLIFE CRISIS LAST — AND WHAT DOES IT MEAN?

Less than one year – not an MLC,
more an MLB (Midlife Blip)

. . . .

Two to three years – you appreciate the chance
to let your ultra-tight belt out a notch or two

. . . .

Five years – it looks like you're enjoying it!

. . . .

Twenty years – it could be embarrassing
buying clothes from the same
shops as your grandchildren

SYMPTOMS YOU CAN SAFELY **IGNORE**

You stay up late each night – if you went to bed you'd just be popping back and forth to the loo

You start fancying much younger celebrities – let's face it, any new celebrity is going to be younger than you

. . . .

You want to swap your glasses for contact lenses – the real reason is that you keep forgetting where you put them

. . . .

You are wearing crotchless underwear – but it turns out these are just old pants that have worn through

WAYS YOU MAY DECIDE TO REINVENT YOURSELF

As a hellraiser – or alternatively
you may just look as though you've
been raised from the dead

. . . .

As a person who should be looked up to
– not as someone who should be looked
up on social media before approaching

. . . .

As 'still younger than a decent whisky'

THE UPSIDE AND THE DOWNSIDE OF NEW CAREERS FOR THE MIDLIFE CRISIS SUFFERER

CAREER CHANGE	UPSIDE	DOWNSIDE
Opening your own pub	You offer customers a well-stocked hostelry	You personally drink the place dry before opening time each day
Opening a bed and breakfast	You get to live in a beautiful location with a range of different visitors	You can't stand any of your visitors and you live miles from anywhere
Counsellor	You can counsel yourself through your MLC	All your fellow-sufferer friends will expect free treatment
Model	It will finally force you to go on that diet	You might be modelling cardies rather than undies

SIGNS TO LOOK FOR IN YOURSELF

You suddenly realise that BMI is not a famous computer company

. . . .

You stop trying to look as good as your favourite celebrities and start trying to make yourself look as good as yourself a few years ago

. . . .

You have become obsessed with the looks of celebrities who are of the same vintage as yourself

When you undo
your trousers, it's
like the ripcord being
pulled on an
inflatable boat

SIGNS TO LOOK FOR IN OTHERS

They suddenly have more luxuriant
hair growth and colour than they
did a couple of years ago

. . . .

Their biscuit tin has been jettisoned
in favour of a smoothie machine

. . . .

They take great delight in spotting any
signs of ageing you have that they don't

. . . .

They use the phrase 'before my
time' to refer to periods which you
know definitely were their time

BAD AND EVEN WORSE DECISIONS YOU MAY BE TEMPTED TO MAKE DURING A MIDLIFE CRISIS

BAD DECISION	EVEN WORSE DECISION
Walking out on your partner of 25 years	Setting up home with a new partner of 25 minutes
Throwing out all your prized personal possessions	Having to pay through the nose to buy them all back on eBay a few weeks later
Keeping your birthdays quiet from now on	Sending back all the cards and presents
Accepting the ageing process and not fighting against it	Dressing like a pensioner and asking people 'do you know how old I am?'

SELF-HELP BOOKS TO HELP YOU DURING YOUR MIDLIFE CRISIS

The Ancient Art of Keeping Your Tummy Held In

How to Change Your Life

. . . .

*How to Change Your Life Back
Again if Things Don't Work Out*

. . . .

*How to Lose Your Hair
But Keep Your Head*

WHAT NOT TO WEAR DURING YOUR MIDLIFE CRISIS – PART ONE

Jeans so tight they will put
onlookers off muffins for life

. . . .

Hipster jeans – especially if it's just
to allow plenty of stomach space

. . . .

Biker jacket – especially if you
only have a pushbike

Everything made of leather – including underpants and socks

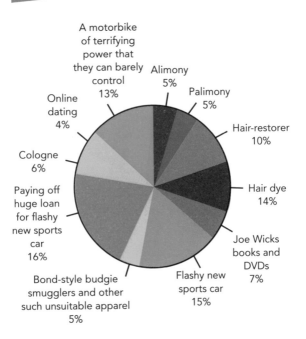

BREAKDOWN OF WHAT MEN SPEND THEIR MONEY ON DURING A MIDLIFE CRISIS

A motorbike of terrifying power that they can barely control
13%

Alimony
5%

Palimony
5%

Online dating
4%

Hair-restorer
10%

Cologne
6%

Hair dye
14%

Paying off huge loan for flashy new sports car
16%

Joe Wicks books and DVDs
7%

Bond-style budgie smugglers and other such unsuitable apparel
5%

Flashy new sports car
15%

WHAT NOT TO WEAR DURING YOUR MIDLIFE CRISIS — PART TWO

A swimsuit so skimpy it gets completely lost under rolls of fat

. . . .

Skintight Lycra to hold your no-longer-skintight skin in place

. . . .

Anything that is still in a size you exceeded at least a decade ago

*Leopard-print
everything –
including contact lenses*

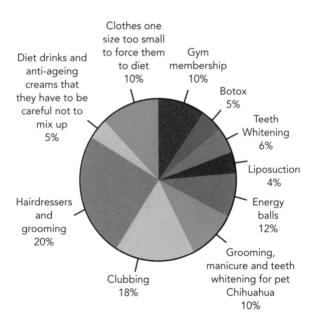

BREAKDOWN OF WHAT WOMEN SPEND THEIR MONEY ON DURING A MIDLIFE CRISIS

Clothes one size too small to force them to diet
10%

Gym membership
10%

Diet drinks and anti-ageing creams that they have to be careful not to mix up
5%

Botox
5%

Teeth Whitening
6%

Liposuction
4%

Energy balls
12%

Hairdressers and grooming
20%

Grooming, manicure and teeth whitening for pet Chihuahua
10%

Clubbing
18%

HOME DECOR FOR THE MIDLIFE CRISIS SUFFERER

A room filled with equipment that can be used either for sado-masochistic delight or osteopathic treatment if you put your back out

. . . .

Nude etchings in every room of your house (and all of them self-portraits)

. . . .

Fairground distorting mirrors to make you look thinner

Posters of ageing film
and rock stars to make
you look younger

MUSICAL INSTRUMENTS YOU MAY DECIDE TO TAKE UP AND WHAT THEY SAY ABOUT YOU

MUSICAL INSTRUMENT	WHAT YOU THINK IT SAYS ABOUT YOU	WHAT IT REALLY SAYS
Electric guitar	You want to express your thrusting sexuality	You have no respect for your next door neighbours
Synthesiser	You want to be a keyboard wizard	You look a bit like Gandalf these days so you're already halfway there
Mouth organ	You will express your midlife angst through the blues	As this will be a five-minute wonder you won't waste too much money

PLACES YOU WILL NOW WANT TO BE SEEN

On the razz rather than on the sofa

. . . .

Backstage with the VIPs rather than in the cheap seats with limited POV

. . . .

Cruising through town past the local nightspots rather than going on a cruise with people with liver spots

. . . .

Behind the wheel of a shiny new car rather than changing the wheel of your old banger

The town centre
rather than
the garden centre

BAD AND EVEN WORSE WAYS OF FLIRTING

BAD WAY OF FLIRTING	EVEN WORSE WAY OF FLIRTING
Nibbling someone's ear	Taking out your teeth and gumming their ear
Trying to present yourself as a sex expert	Presenting a history lecture on the changes in sex you have seen during your lifetime
Giving someone a poke on Facebook	Giving someone a poke while standing behind them on a crowded bus
Asking someone if they'd like to join you in a game of strip poker	When they tell you no thanks, playing a game of strip solitaire on your own in front of them

PROBLEMS ARISING FROM LOOKING UP EX-PARTNERS

They will now look as old as you
and may be having an even more
severe MLC than you are

. . . .

Their current partners may be bigger
than you and/or psychotic

. . . .

If you find a room in their house
entirely covered in pictures of
yourself, make a quick getaway!

If their online profile pic shows them in prison garb, this might explain why you haven't seen them for a few years

facebook
LOCATION : PRISON
HOBBIES : BREAKING, ENTERING, WRONGDOING...

ADVANTAGES AND DISADVANTAGES OF TAKING UP WITH A YOUNGER PARTNER

ADVANTAGE	DISADVANTAGE
Their youthful energy will help you to rediscover life	Their youthful energy will cause you to have a cardiac arrest
They will help you upgrade to all the latest technology	They will upgrade you for a more modern up-to-date model at any time
They will be more in touch with the latest fashions	Because of this they won't be seen in public with you
They will challenge your increasingly reactionary views	They might challenge some of them in a court of law

WHAT ANIMALS WOULD DO IF THEY HAD A MIDLIFE CRISIS

Rhinos – spend an absolute fortune on Botox to fill out those wrinkles

. . . .

Sphynx cats – invest in extravagant hairpieces

. . . .

Gorillas – apply a bit of hair dye to the silverback

Bald eagle —
comb the feathers
over the top

SIGNS YOU MAY BE HAVING YOUR MIDLIFE CRISIS EARLY

You can actually fit into those
skinny jeans you bought to make
yourself feel more youthful

. . . .

You need a magnifying glass to see
where to apply your anti-wrinkle cream

. . . .

You still have acne on the places you are
planning to have cosmetic surgery

YOU HAVE DIFFICULTY FINDING ANY PATCHES WHERE YOU NEED TO APPLY HAIR RESTORER

SIGNS YOU MAY NEVER HAVE A MIDLIFE CRISIS

You can wear comfy old cardigans
without a scintilla of shame

• • • • • • • • • •

When you look in the mirror you see
someone who is mature, wise and
distinguished rather than someone who
is old, wrinkled and extinguished

• • • • • • • • • •

Your eyesight is so bad you can't see
yourself clearly enough in the mirror
to notice any signs of ageing

• • • • • • • • • •

You never really matured in the first place

THINGS A MIDLIFER MAY HAVE IN THEIR HOME

A rowing machine (unused)

. . . .

A large pot of anti-wrinkle
cream (almost empty)

. . . .

A library of dieting and self-
help books (many unread)

An electric guitar
(hopelessly out of tune)

PROBLEMS WITH VEHICLES FAVOURED BY MIDLIFE CRISIS SUFFERERS

VEHICLE	PROBLEM
Bright pink car with eyelashes on the headlights	It will look like your car is also having a hot flush
Massive shiny Harley Davidson motorbike	You may need a winch to haul you up onto the seat – like a knight from days of yore!
Super-fast open-top sports car	It will play havoc with your now flyaway hair
Your 'get healthy' racing bike	It will sit untouched and unloved in your garage between September and June

PEOPLE WHO WILL NEVER HAVE A MIDLIFE CRISIS

Rich people who spend most of
their money on trying to look young
even when they are quite young

. . . .

People with young children – not only are
they permanently too tired to have an MLC,
but their kids would just laugh at them

. . . .

Children's TV presenters – with their
brash bright clothes and hyperactive,
overenthusiastic personalities, having a
midlife crisis wouldn't make much difference

Character actors who have been made up to look old so many times they've forgotten what they actually should look like or how old they are

HOW YOU THINK YOU LOOK AND HOW YOU LOOK TO OTHERS

THINK YOU LOOK	LOOK TO OTHERS
Could be mistaken for a 29-year-old	Could be mistaken for a 29-year-old cheese
Keeping up with the latest fashions	Keeping up your sagging belly by sheer will power
Bronzed all over	Like you've walked out of a sepia-tinged photo
Exuding energy and enthusiasm	Sweaty and in imminent danger of cardiac arrest

WAYS THE MIDLIFER CAN HIDE SIGNS OF AGEING

A hair transplant that leaves
you with a fringe so extreme it
completely obscures your face

. . . .

Sunglasses that hide your baggy old eyes
but fool everyone into thinking you just
jetted in from some exotic location

. . . .

Lots of jewellery so shiny it will
reflect the light and prevent anyone
looking at you too closely

TO AVOID ANYONE
GETTING A CHANCE
TO FOCUS ON
HOW OLD YOU'RE
LOOKING, KEEP
MOVING CONSTANTLY
— PREFERABLY INTO
THE DISTANCE

ADVISABLE AND INADVISABLE COSMETIC SURGERY

ADVISABLE	INADVISABLE
Having your teeth whitened	Ending up looking like you've switched your full beam headlights on each time you grin
Having the bags under your eyes removed	Leaving yourself permanently unable to blink
Dyeing your greying hair	Shaving your head to avoid the cost of dyeing every few weeks
Having your lips filled	Insisting your beautician uses the full tube of filler so you end up with wonky lips

HOW TO DENY YOU'RE HAVING
A MIDLIFE CRISIS

'That leather jacket on my coat hook must have been left behind by one of the grandchildren'

'I'm only listening to gangsta rap as research for my Open University sociology course'

. . . .

'I wear a padded bra to keep my chest warm – that's also the reason for my boob job'

. . . .

'My hair has naturally turned sheer black'

HOLIDAYS THAT MIGHT BE A GIVEAWAY

That dirty weekender in Ibiza

. . . .

Any resort that keeps getting the 'definitely not family-friendly' comments on TripAdvisor

. . . .

Two weeks at a theme park riding roller coasters all day every day regardless of what it does to your bad back

A few weeks lazing on a nudist beach – only to discover everyone else there is older and in even worse condition than you

ADVISABLE AND INADVISABLE LEISURE ACTIVITIES FOR THE MIDLIFER

ADVISABLE	INADVISABLE
Going to the gym occasionally	Training to join the Olympic weightlifting team
Listening to some more up-to-date music	Becoming the DJ at local all-nighters
Jogging round the park each day	Sleeping on a park bench each night
Using social media to meet interesting new people	Finding interesting new things about people you already know by hacking into their computers

MIDLIFERS IN HISTORY

HENRY VIII – Kept trading his wives in for younger models (don't get any ideas, chaps)

. . . .

CALIGULA – he devoted his life to one long, extremely debauched toga party

. . . .

LUCREZIA BORGIA – Poisoning, murder, multiple marriages – now that's what we call a midlife crisis!

BOADICEA –
Fed up with being a
stay-at-home housewife,
she revved up her chariot
(an ancient version
of the MLC sports car)
and took on the Romans

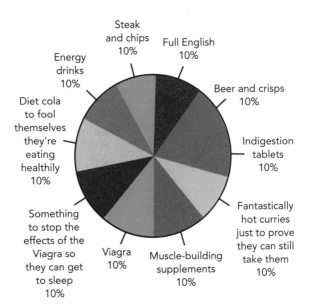

BREAKDOWN OF A MAN'S DAILY FOOD AND DRINK INTAKE DURING HIS MIDLIFE CRISIS

Steak and chips
10%

Full English
10%

Energy drinks
10%

Beer and crisps
10%

Diet cola to fool themselves they're eating healthily
10%

Indigestion tablets
10%

Something to stop the effects of the Viagra so they can get to sleep
10%

Viagra
10%

Muscle-building supplements
10%

Fantastically hot curries just to prove they can still take them
10%

BREAKDOWN OF A WOMAN'S DAILY FOOD AND DRINK INTAKE DURING HER MIDLIFE CRISIS

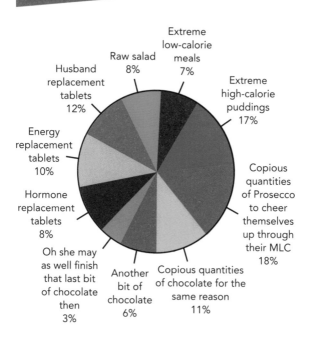

Raw salad
8%

Extreme low-calorie meals
7%

Husband replacement tablets
12%

Extreme high-calorie puddings
17%

Energy replacement tablets
10%

Copious quantities of Prosecco to cheer themselves up through their MLC
18%

Hormone replacement tablets
8%

Oh she may as well finish that last bit of chocolate then
3%

Another bit of chocolate
6%

Copious quantities of chocolate for the same reason
11%

HOW YOU WILL KNOW
YOUR MIDLIFE CRISIS IS
FINALLY OVER

When you are too
embarrassed to ask if
your new Ray-Bans
can be fitted with
trifocal lenses

When you catch sight of your sagging
belly in a mirror and don't care any more

. . . .

When you can laugh at yourself
before anyone else does

. . . .

When you realise that all your efforts
to look younger have in fact made
you look considerably older

THE BAD NEWS ABOUT YOUR MIDLIFE CRISIS BEING OVER

You are now officially past middle age

. . . .

What's next – an Old-Life Crisis?

. . . .

If you still look weird, you've
no longer got an excuse

THE EFFORT AND
EXPENSE REQUIRED TO
MAKE YOURSELF LOOK
YOUNGER IS NOW
BEYOND YOU, UNLESS
YOU QUALIFY FOR A
GOVERNMENT GRANT

THE GOOD NEWS ABOUT YOUR MIDLIFE CRISIS BEING OVER

You will save a fortune on lotions, potions and rather foolish fashion choices

. . . .

You can now finally relax and enjoy life. Leather trousers – who needs them?

. . . .

You can hang on to your sporty car by claiming it's a pimped-up mobility scooter

Rather than fighting
the ravages of time,
you can use them to
your advantage and
get young people to
do things for you

A PHILOSOPHICAL VIEW

Getting older is a hell of a lot
better than the alternative

. . . .

If I cared what I look like I
wouldn't look like this!

. . . .

You are only as old as you feel
– although it may help if you're
being felt in a darkened room

IF YOU CAN KEEP YOUR WRINKLES WHEN ALL THOSE AROUND YOU ARE LOSING THEIRS, YOU WILL SAVE A FORTUNE ON COSMETIC PROCEDURES

If you're interested in finding out more about our books, find us on Facebook at **Summersdale Publishers** and follow us on Twitter at **@Summersdale**.

www.summersdale.com